THE GREATEST RESCUE

Jesus has come to the rescue! How? He came to this earth to save sinners like you and me. God the Father's plan was to send Jesus, his Son, to this earth to die on the cross and take the punishment for sin. All people sin. Sin is the things that we do, say and think that are against God and his commands. Jesus lived a perfect life, free of sin and then by his death on the cross he ensured that all those who trust in him as their Saviour, will have their sins forgiven and receive everlasting life. This is certainly the greatest rescue ever.

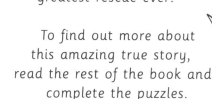

To find out more about this amazing true story, read the rest of the book and complete the puzzles.

This story can be found towards the end of the gospels of Matthew, Mark, Luke and John in the New Testament.

Turn the page to find some puzzles that will tell you more about Jesus' friends and his enemies.

CRACK THE CODE

Jesus was born in Bethlehem and grew up in Nazareth. He was a normal child – except for a couple of things. He didn't sin and he was both God and human. When he was a grown-up, Jesus began to go around the country of Israel telling people about God, his Father. Some people began to follow him. They had a special name.

The letters for this word have mysteriously changed into numbers. Can you work out what letters should be here instead, using the code below?

4 9 19 3 9 16 12 5 19   _ _ _ _ _ _ _ _ _

A	B	C	D	E	F	G	H	I	J	K	L	M
1	2	3	4	5	6	7	8	9	10	11	12	13

N	O	P	Q	R	S	T	U	V	W	X	Y	Z
14	15	16	17	18	19	20	21	22	23	24	25	26

Jesus had enemies as well as friends. To find out the name of one group of enemies break the code below. Write down the first letter of each picture.

_ _ _ _ _ _ _ _

UNJUMBLE THE LETTERS ...

The Pharisees and the chief priests were jealous of him. They didn't believe he was the Son of God. They didn't like the words he said or the things he did. Secretly, they began to plot how to kill him. What amazing things did Jesus do? To work some of them out, unjumble the letters and then put the words in the right place.

deealh, tghtau, thitoryau, desiar, ddea

He _ _ _ _ _ _ people. (Matthew 12:15)

He _ _ _ _ _ _ with _ _ _ _ _ _ _ _ _. (Matthew 21:23)

He _ _ _ _ _ _ people from the _ _ _ _. (John 11:43-44)

But even though Jesus did these wonderful things the Pharisees still hated him.

SPOT THE DIFFERENCE

Can you spot the six differences between these two pictures?

When Jesus brought a man called Lazarus back from the dead the Pharisees got even angrier. They wanted to kill Lazarus too.

Anyone who saw Jesus was to go straight to the Pharisees with the news so that they could arrest him.

Jerusalem was a dangerous place for Jesus to be. But the Passover Feast was soon going to take place there. It was a special feast that all the Jews celebrated. Jesus knew that it was important for him to be there. It was God's plan for Jesus to die instead of sinners. Jesus knew that it was God's plan for him to die in Jerusalem.

Follow the letters around the grid on the opposite page to find out what Jesus said would happen to him:

FOLLOW THE LETTERS ...

→

S	e	e	w	e	a	r	e	g	o	i	n	g	u	p	t
e	S	o	n	o	f	M	a	n	b	y	t	h	e	p	o
h	e	l	i	v	e	r	e	d	o	v	e	r	t	r	J
t	d	h	a	m	e	f	u	l	l	y	t	r	o	o	e
t	e	s	h	i	r	d	d	a	y	h	e	e	t	p	r
u	b	d	t	s	u	n	d	e	r	s	w	a	h	h	u
o	l	n	e	e	s	e	t	h	i	t	i	t	e	e	s
b	l	a	h	l	e	18	:	31	n	o	l	e	G	t	a
a	i	d	t	p	h	e	34	-	g	o	l	d	e	s	l
n	w	e	n	i	t	k	u	L	s	d	r	a	n	w	e
e	e	k	o	c	f	o	e	n	o	n	i	n	t	i	m
t	h	c	d	s	i	d	e	h	T	e	s	d	i	l	a
t	r	o	n	A	n	o	p	u	t	i	p	s	l	l	n
i	o	m	e	b	l	l	i	w	d	n	a	s	e	b	d
r	F	d	e	h	s	i	l	p	m	o	c	c	a	e	e
w	s	i	t	a	h	t	g	n	i	h	t	y	r	e	v

↓ ↑ ← →

_ _ _, _, _ _ _ _ _ _ _ _ _ _ _

_ _

_ _. _ _ _ _ _ _ _ _ _ _

_ _

_ _.

_ _. _ _ _

_ _.

_ _ _ _ _ _:_ _ - _ _.

Mirror Image

Six days before the Passover Feast, Jesus was with some of his friends — a man called Lazarus and his sisters, Martha and Mary. They were eating together. Mary took some expensive perfume and poured it over Jesus' feet. The smell of the perfume filled the whole house. One of Jesus' disciples, Judas, was annoyed. He said, 'That perfume could have been sold and given to the poor. It was worth a year's wages!' Why was Judas so interested in the money?

Read these letters in a mirror and you will find out what Judas was really like.

Judas was a thief.

— — — — — — — — — — — — — — — — — —

To find out what Jesus said, follow the words around the house and fill in the blanks on the next page.

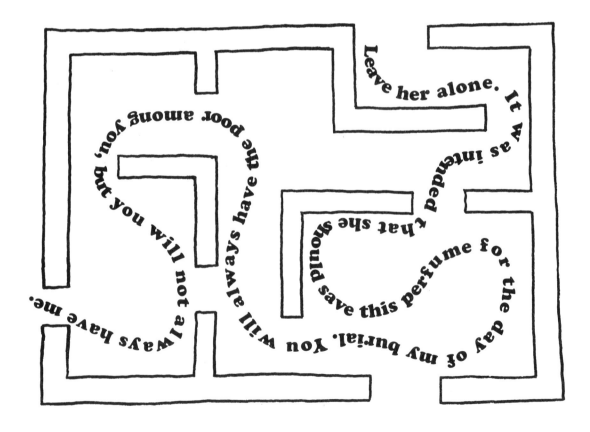

_ _ _ _ _ _ _ _ _ _ _ _ _. _ _ _ _ _ _ _ _

_ _ _ _ _ _ _ _ _ _ _ _ _ _ _ _ _ _

_ _ _ _ _ _ _ _ _ _ _ _ _ _. _ _ _ _ _ _ _

_ _ _ _ _ _ _ _ _ _ _ _ _ _ _ _ _ _ _,

_ _ _ _ _ _ _ _ _ _ _ _ _ _ _ _ _ _.

Jesus knew that he was going to die soon.

He entered into the city of Jerusalem riding on a donkey that had never been ridden before. People came out to greet him. They were carrying palm branches and they were all shouting:

_ _ _ _ _ _ _

Unjumble these words to find out what they said next.

Is blessed who he in comes name the the of Lord

_ _

_ _ _ _ _ _ _ _ _ _.

SOLVE THE JIGSAW PUZZLE

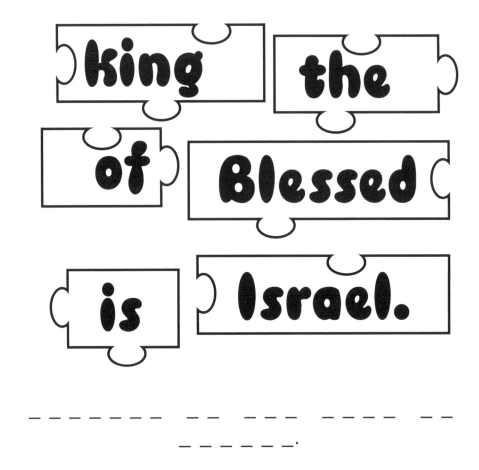

king   the   of   Blessed   is   Israel.

_ _ _ _ _ _   _ _   _ _ _   _ _ _ _   _ _

_ _ _ _ _ _.

Jesus had an evening meal with his disciples one night. He felt troubled. Why was he troubled? Tick the correct answer.

1. Had he lost his sandals?
2. Did he forget to buy bread?
3. Perhaps he knew that a friend was going to betray him?

Jesus said that whoever he gave his bread to would be the one to betray him. Who did he give it to? Take each letter on the next page and go back one letter in the alphabet to find out who it was.

FIND THE NAME

KVEBT JTDBSJPU

_ _ _ _ _   _ _ _ _ _ _ _ _

What did Judas do when he took the bread? Piece together the picture squares to find out.

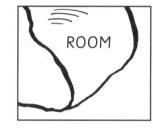

_ _   _ _ _ _   _ _ _   _ _ _ _ _

Jesus told the others that he would soon go to a place where they would not be allowed to follow. Peter was confused. 'Why can't I follow you?' he asked. 'I will lay down my life for you.'

Find out what Jesus said in reply. Fit the shapes to the words.

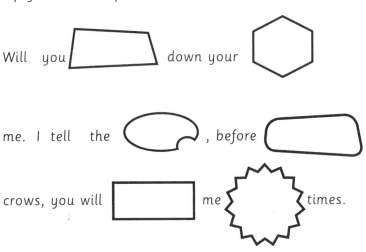

Will you ⬚ down your ⬡

me. I tell the ⬭ , before ▢

crows, you will ▭ me ✴ times.

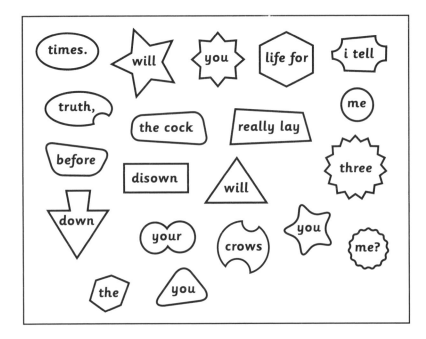

After this, Jesus and his disciples went to an olive grove. Judas knew where they were going so he took some Pharisees there and some soldiers of the high priest.

Find out what the soldiers were carrying by following the dotted lines.

_____, _____ and _____

Judas needed to show the soldiers who they should arrest. So he went up and gave Jesus a kiss. The disciples saw that Jesus was about to be arrested. What did Peter do? Put a tick beside the correct answer.

* Run away
* Hide Jesus
* Cut off one of the guard's ears

Jesus told Peter to put his sword away. Jesus was taken away to be questioned by the chief priests and the Pharisees. He was beaten and made fun of. The soldiers blindfolded him. They then hit him on the face and asked him a question.

PR _ PHESY! WH _ HIT Y _ U?

There is one letter missing from this sentence. See if you can work out what it is?

When all this was going on Peter was speaking to people outside the high priest's house. Three times he was asked if he was one of Jesus' disciples. Three times Peter said that he wasn't. He even said that he didn't know Jesus. When Peter denied Jesus for a third time something happened...

It happened just as Jesus had said it would. When the cock crowed Peter turned and saw Jesus looking at him. He realised what an awful thing he had done. Peter ran out of the courtyard and wept bitterly.

Here we have a pretend newspaper from Bible times. Can you work out which picture and which title has been torn out? Match the pictures opposite with the shapes below. The newspaper story will give you a clue.

The Bible Times

TODAY'S NEWS

MATCH THE SHAPES

MYSTERIOUS DEATH OF COCKEREL!

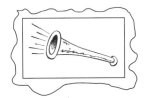

WHO BLEW THE TRUMPET?

WHY DID THE COCKEREL CROW THREE TIMES?

The Bible Times

TODAY'S NEWS

Shock news today. Jesus has been betrayed, arrested and even one of his closest disciples has denied ever having known him! Jesus predicted that Peter would deny him three times and it has happened. That is why the cockerel crowed. Jesus said that when Peter had denied him three times this would happen and it did. Peter is very upset that he has treated Jesus in this way.

Jesus was questioned by lots of people. The chief priests questioned him and then sent him to Pilate, the Roman Governor. Pilate questioned him and then sent him to King Herod. Herod was really pleased. He had wanted to meet Jesus for himself. But when Jesus didn't answer any of his questions, Herod and his soldiers made fun of him and dressed him in an elegant robe as a joke. Then Herod sent him back to Pilate. Pilate offered to release Jesus. But the crowd did not want this. To find out what they said, put the words in the right order on the next page.

ARRANGE THE WORDS

Arrange the words above in the spaces below.

_ _ _ _ _ _ _ _ _ _ _ _ _ _ _!

_ _ _ _ _ _ _ _ _ _ _ _ _ _ _ _ _ _

_ _. _ _ _ _ _ _ _ _ _!

_ _ _ _ _ _ _ _ _ _!

Who was Barabbas? Was he a brave hero? Was he a mighty warrior? Was he a popular entertainer? No, he was a wicked robber... but the people wanted to kill Jesus and not Barabbas.

Pilate then took Jesus away and had him _ _ _ _ _ _ _.

The soldiers put a _ _ _ _ _ _ _ _ _ _ _ _ _ on his head.

They clothed him in a purple _ _ _ _ and made fun of him,

saying, 'Hail King of the Jews.'

They _ _ _ _ _ _ _ him in the face. _ _ _ _ _ _ _ asked

the crowd, 'Shall I _ _ _ _ _ _ _ _ your king?'

The _ _ _ _ _ replied – 'We have no king but

_ _ _ _ _ _ !

Even Pilate's _ _ _ _ tried to warn him not to harm Jesus.

But he didn't listen to her. He listened to the _ _ _ _ _

instead.

_ _ _ _ _ _ handed Jesus over to be _ _ _ _ _ _ _ _ _.

Jesus had to carry his own cross through the city. But at one point the cross got so heavy a man called Joseph of Arimathea was pulled out of the crowd to carry Jesus' cross for him.

When they reached Golgotha, the Place of a Skull, Jesus was nailed to the cross. He was crucified with one criminal on either side of him. Read the following words backwards to find out what was written on the sign above Jesus' cross, then write it on the sign.

Jesus of Nazareth, King of the Jews.

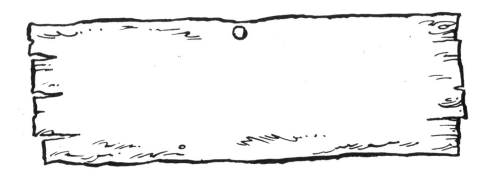

When the soldiers crucified Jesus they took his clothes and divided them into four shares – one for each of them. But his undergarment was not torn. Instead they gambled to see who would get it. Another prophecy came true. Put the words below in the correct order to find out what it was.

among   my   cast   divided

for   They   garments   and

clothing   lots   my   them

____ _____ __ _____ ____ ____ ___

____ ____ ___ __ _____.

A prophecy is a message from God. It was sometimes about something that would happen in the future. Many prophecies about Jesus from the Old Testament have now come true.

While he was on the cross, people mocked and insulted Jesus. One of the criminals yelled at him – 'If you really are God's promised Messiah save yourself and us.' But the other thief stuck up for Jesus. He was sorry for his sins and he knew that he deserved to die. But Jesus didn't deserve to suffer and die. The good thief realised that Jesus was who he said he was – the Son of God. To find out what this thief said to Jesus follow the words around the star. To find out what Jesus said in reply, follow the wiggly line below – but backwards.

The thief on the cross said, 'Jesus, remember me when you come into your kingdom.'

___ _____ ____ __ ___ _____ ____ '_____ _____ __

____ ___ ____ ____ ____ _____.'

'paradise in me with be will you today, truth the you tell I

_ ____ ___ ___ _____,' _____ ___ ____ __ ____ __

__ _____.

BREAK THE CODE

When he was on the cross Jesus said seven important things. To find out what these were – break the code below.

A	B	C	D	E	F	G	H	I	J	K	L	M
1	2	3	4	5	6	7	8	9	10	11	12	13

N	O	P	Q	R	S	T	U	V	W	X	Y	Z
14	15	16	17	18	19	20	21	22	23	24	25	26

1. Here is your _ _ _. Here is your _ _ _ _ _ _.
(19,15,14/ 13,15,20,8,5,18))
This showed that Jesus loved his mother and cared for her.

2. I am _ _ _ _ _ _ _. (20,8,9,18,19,20,25)
This shows us that Jesus was human and that he suffered.

3. Father _ _ _ _ _ _ _ them for they do not _ _ _ _ what they are
_ _ _ _ _ . (6,15,18,7,9,22,5/ 11,14,15,23/ 4,15,9,14,7)
This shows Jesus' love for his enemies.

4. I tell you the _ _ _ _ _ .   _ _ _ _ _ you will be with _ _ in
Paradise. (20,18,21,20,8/ 20,15,4,1,25/ 13,5)
These words show us that when someone who trusts in Jesus dies
they go to heaven immediately. They don't have to wait.

5. My _ _ _. _ _ God. Why have you _ _ _ _ _ _ _ _ me?
(7,15,4/ 13,25/ 6,15,18,19,1,11,5,14)
This shows us that even God the Father abandoned Jesus. Jesus was totally alone.

6. It is _ _ _ _ _ _ _ _. (6,9,14,9,19,8,5,4)
This shows us that when Jesus died on the cross, he finished God's plan to save sinners. Nothing else needs to be done.

7. Father into your _ _ _ _ _ I commit my _ _ _ _ _ _.
(8,1,14,4,19/ 19,16,9,18,9,20)
This shows us that it wasn't his enemies that killed him. Jesus chose to die just when he had done everything that was needed.

After Jesus had said these things he died. But that wasn't the end. Just at the point when Jesus died, the curtain in the temple was torn from the top to the bottom. This showed people that although their sin kept them separate from God, with Jesus' death this separation was no longer needed. We can now come to God through Jesus Christ to have our sins forgiven.

There was also a great earthquake and the graves opened. The bodies of many godly people who had died came back to life again.

While all this was happening the Roman soldiers came to inspect the bodies. The thieves were still alive so they killed them by breaking their bones. But when they came to Jesus they found that he was already dead, so they left him alone. One soldier pierced Jesus' side with a spear to check that he was really dead. He was. This all fulfilled a prophecy from the Old Testament. To find out what the prophecy is, do the wordsearch on the next page. Put the letters that are left over into the gaps and you'll have the prophecy!

WORDSEARCH

Barabbas
God
Thorns
Truth
Torn
Betray
Crucified
Pilate
Crucify

Nails
Donkey
Mother
Curtain
Christ
Peter
Forgive
Crown

Repent
Pharisees
Mary
Resurrection
Purple
Robe
Die
Holy

c	u	r	t	a	i	n	n	o	t	o	n	e	o	b
r	e	s	u	r	r	e	c	t	i	o	n	f	h	a
u	i	s	b	o	t	o	r	n	n	e	s	w	i	r
c	h	r	i	s	t	p	u	r	p	l	e	l	e	a
i	b	e	t	r	a	y	c	l	i	b	e	t	e	b
f	o	r	g	i	v	e	i	b	l	r	e	b	o	b
i	k	e	n	t	h	e	f	y	a	p	o	w	i	a
e	l	l	m	m	a	r	y	t	t	r	u	t	h	s
d	i	e	o	l	o	o	n	k	e	o	n	t	o	h
e	o	n	t	e	t	e	h	e	y	n	a	i	l	s
h	a	v	h	e	p	p	c	r	o	w	n	i	y	e
r	c	e	e	e	d	t	h	o	r	n	s	g	o	d
p	h	a	r	i	s	e	e	s	y	e	k	n	o	d

Answer

Two men, Joseph of Arimathea and Nicodemus, were friends of Jesus. They took Jesus' body down from the cross and buried it in a brand new tomb. The following day was the special day of rest for the Jewish people. But the day after that the women, who followed Jesus, came to the tomb to anoint Jesus' body with perfumes and spices.

SPOT THE DIFFERENCE

Can you spot the six differences between these two pictures? There are some deliberate mistakes. Which picture do you think is the right one.

When they arrived the women found an empty tomb and the stone that kept the tomb closed, had been rolled away. It was still early in the morning, but Jesus' body was nowhere to be found.

Suddenly two men, in clothes that gleamed like lightning, appeared beside them. The women were frightened.

The angels asked them, Why do you look for the _ _ _ _ _ _ among

the _ _ _ _ ? He is not here; he has _ _ _ _ _!'

The women ran back to tell the disciples, but the disciples didn't believe them. Peter and John ran to the tomb to see for themselves. The tomb was empty just as the women had said. When Peter and John returned, Mary Magdalene stayed behind. She looked in the tomb and saw two angels there. They asked her why she was crying. Look in a mirror to find out what Mary said,

They have taken my Lord away and I don't know where they have put him.

_ _ _ _ _ _ _ _ _ _ _ _ _ _ _ _ _ _ _ _ _ _ _ _ _ _ _ _ _ _ _ _ _ _ _
_ _ _ _ _ _ _ _ _ _ _ _ _ _ _ _ _ _ _.

Just then Jesus appeared, but Mary didn't recognise him. Who did Mary think Jesus was? Follow the letters around the garden and you will find out. Write down only the letters that are in the circles – ignore the others.

_ _ _ _ _ _ _ _

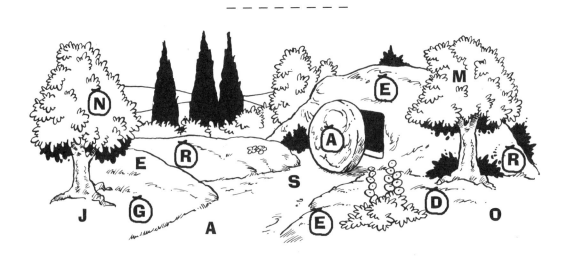

FOLLOW THE DOVES ...

Jesus had risen from the dead. He really was alive. After that Jesus appeared to some of the disciples. They were hiding in a locked room because they were so scared. But Jesus suddenly appeared in the room. What did he say to the disciples? Follow the flying doves to find out.

– – – – – – – – – – – – – –.

Thomas wasn't there, however, and didn't believe the others when they said they'd seen Jesus. He said 'Unless I see the nail marks in his hands and put my finger where the nails were, and put my hand into his side, I will not believe it.'

When Jesus appeared to the disciples for a second time, Thomas was there. Jesus told him to put his finger where the nails had been and to touch his side. Stop doubting and believe, Jesus told him. But Thomas didn't need to do that – he believed. Jesus said to him, 'Because you have seen me, you have believed; blessed are those who have not seen and yet have believed.'

People who are alive today have not seen Jesus face to face like his disciples did, but we can still believe in him. God's Holy Spirit changes us on the inside so that we can trust the Lord Jesus to forgive us for our sins. We can believe in him and in God's great rescue plan for sinners. Jesus remained on the earth for a few weeks after his resurrection and then he went up to heaven. That is where he is today with God, his Father. One day he is coming back. On that day those who trust in him will also rise from the dead as he did and go to heaven to be with him forever.

Answers

Page 2   Disciples / Pharisees

Page 3   He healed people. / He taught with authority. / He raised people from the dead.

Page 4   Day/night, 3 people/2 people, cat/mouse, feather pen/no feather pen, picture/candle, striped robe/checked robe.

Page 5   See, we are going up to Jerusalem and everything that is written about the Son of Man by the prophets will be accomplished. For he will be delivered over to the Gentiles and will be mocked and shamefully treated and spit upon. And on the third day he will rise. The disciples understood none of these things. Luke 18:31-34

Page 6   Judas was a thief.

Page 7   Leave her alone. It was intended that she should save this perfume for the day of my burial. You will always have the poor among you, but you will not always have me.
Hosanna. / Blessed is he who comes in the name of the Lord.

Page 8   Blessed is the king of Israel / (3).

Page 9   Judas Iscariot / He left the room.

Page 10 Will you really lay down your life for me. I tell you the truth, before the cock crows, you will disown me three times.

Page 11 Swords, torches and lanterns / Cut of one of the guard's ears / Prophesy! Who hit you?

Page 12 Why did the cockerel crow three times? / picture of cockerel.

Page 14 Away with this man! Release Barabbas to us. Crucify him! Crucify him!

Page 15 Flogged/whipped, crown of thorns, robe, struck, Pilate, crucify, crowd, Caesar, wife, crowd, Pilate, crucified.

Page 16 Jesus of Nazareth, King of the Jews / They divided my garments among them and cast lots for my clothing.

Page 17 The thief on the cross said, 'Jesus, remember me when you come into your kingdom.' / I tell you the truth, today you will be with me in paradise.

Page 18 (1) Son/mother, (2) thirsty, (3) forgive/know/doing, (4) truth/today/me,

Page 19 (5) God/my/forsaken, (6) finished, (7) hands/spirit.

Page 20 Not one of his bones will be broken. They will look on the one they have pierced.

Page 21 Day/night, two women/three women, soldier/angel, no bird/bird, dog/no dog, closed tomb/open tomb.
The first picture.

Page 22 Living, dead, risen / They have taken my Lord away and I don't know where they have put him/ Gardener.

Page 23 Peace be with you.

10 9 8 7 6 5 4 3 2 1
Text by Catherine Mackenzie
Illustrations by Tim Charnick
ISBN 978-1-84550-617-9
© 2011 Christian Focus Publications

Published by Christian Focus Publications,
Geanies House, Fearn,
Ross-shire, IV20 1TW, Scotland, U.K.
Printed and bound by Bell and Bain, Glasgow

Mixed Sources
Product group from well-managed forests and other controlled sources
www.fsc.org Cert no. TT-COC-002769
© 1996 Forest Stewardship Council
FSC

The text and answers are based on the New International Version and English Standard Version of the Bible.